Let us press on to know the Lord.
His going forth is as certain as the dawn;
and He will come to us like the rain,
like the spring rain watering the earth.
Hosea 6:3, NASB

FOCUS ON THE FAMILY

renewing the heart

Spiritual Refreshment for Each New Day

TYNDALE HOUSE PUBLISHERS, INC.
WHEATON, ILLINOIS

Visit Tyndale's exciting Web site at www.tyndale.com

Cover design by Paetzold Design
Interior design by Jackie Noe

Hymn portions are from *The One Year Book of Hymns,* © 1995 by Robert K. Brown and Mark R. Norton (Tyndale House Publishers, Inc.) and are used by permission of Tyndale House Publishers, Inc.

Scripture quotations marked KJV are taken from the *Holy Bible,* King James Version.

Scripture quotations marked NASB are taken from the *New American Standard Bible,* © 1960, 1962, 1963, 1968, 1971, 1972, 1973, 1975, 1977 by The Lockman Foundation. Used by permission.

Scripture quotations marked NIV are taken from the *Holy Bible,* New International Version®. NIV®. Copyright © 1973, 1978, 1984 by International Bible Society. Used by permission of Zondervan Publishing House. All rights reserved.

Scripture quotations marked "NKJV" are taken from the New King James Version. Copyright © 1979, 1980, 1982 by Thomas Nelson, Inc. Used by permission. All rights reserved.

Quotes marked Debra Evans, *Kindred Hearts* are taken from *Kindred Hearts,* copyright © 1997 by Debra Evans (Focus on the Family Publishing) and are used by permission of Focus on the Family.

Quotes marked Dr. Deborah Newman, *Then God Created Woman* are taken from *Then God Created Woman,* copyright © 1997 by Deborah Newman (Focus on the Family Publishing) and are used by permission of Focus on the Family.

Quotes marked Susan Miller, *After the Boxes Are Unpacked* are taken from *After the Boxes Are Unpacked,* copyright © 1995 by Susan Miller (Focus on the Family Publishing) and are used by permission of Focus on the Family.

Quotes marked Patsy Clairmont, *Under His Wings* are taken from *Under His Wings,* copyright © 1994 by Patsy Clairmont (Focus on the Family Publishing) and are used by permission of Focus on the Family.

Quotes marked Chuck Snyder, *Men* are taken from *Men: Some Assembly Required,* copyright © 1995 by Chuck Snyder (Focus on the Family Publishing) and are used by permission of Focus on the Family.

ISBN 0-8423-5293-7

Printed in the United States of America.

04   03   02   01   00   99
7   6   5   4   3   2

Renewing the Heart books and conferences seek to honor the Lord as they equip the saints through sound, scriptural teaching; encourage the weary through praise, worship, humor, and fellowship; and evangelize the lost by presenting the saving gospel of Jesus Christ.

$\mathcal{G}$OD WANTS YOU TO HAVE CHRISTIAN FRIENDS—FRIENDS WHO CAN PUT THEIR ARMS AROUND YOU AND REMIND YOU THAT YOU ARE LOVED. FRIENDS WHO CAN ENCOURAGE YOU. FRIENDS WHO REFLECT HIS LOVE FOR YOU IN A VISIBLE WAY. FRIENDS WHO ARE AN EXTENSION OF JESUS CHRIST, NOT A SUBSTITUTE FOR HIM. Susan Miller, *After the Boxes Are Unpacked*

Therefore encourage one another, and build up one another.
1 THESSALONIANS 5:11, NASB

ℱOR ALL THE BLESSINGS OF THE YEAR

For all the blessings of the year,
For all the friends we hold so dear,
For peace on earth, both far and near,
We thank Thee, O Lord.

For love of Thine, which never tires,
Which all our better thought inspires,
And warms our lives with heavenly fires,
We thank Thee, O Lord.

ALBERT H. HUTCHINSON (N.D.)

If Thou But Suffer God to Guide Thee

If thou but suffer God to guide thee,

And hope in Him through all thy ways,

He'll give thee strength, whate'er betide thee,

And bear thee through the evil days;

Who trusts in God's unchanging love

Builds on the Rock that nought can move.

GEORG NEUMARK (1621–1681)

TRANSLATED BY CATHERINE WINKWORTH (1827–1878)

MEEKNESS DOESN'T MEAN WEAKNESS BUT STRENGTH UNDER GOD'S CONTROL. IT'S A SERENITY OF SPIRIT THAT ACCEPTS EVERYTHING THAT COMES INTO OUR LIVES AS BEING ALLOWED BY GOD, WHETHER WE THINK IT'S GOOD OR BAD. THIS ENABLES US TO GO *THROUGH* TRIALS IN A GOD-HONORING WAY. Chuck Snyder, *Men*

Your attitude should be the same as that of Christ Jesus:
Who, being in very nature God, did not consider equality with God something
to be grasped, but made himself nothing, taking the very nature of a servant,
being made in human likeness. And being found in appearance as a man,
he humbled himself and became obedient to death—even death on a cross!
PHILIPPIANS 2:5-8, NIV

Softly and Tenderly Jesus Is Calling

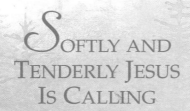

Softly and tenderly Jesus is calling,

Calling for you and for me;

See, on the portals He's waiting

and watching,

Watching for you and for me.

Come home, come home,

Ye who are weary, come home;

Earnestly, tenderly, Jesus is calling,

Calling, O sinner, come home!

WILLIAM LAMARTINE THOMPSON

(1847–1909)

When we won't let ourselves be held in the midst of our messes by the God who loves us and made us, we miss the unspeakable joy of knowing that we are truly His beloved.

Dr. Deborah Newman, *Then God Created Woman*

I have loved you with an everlasting love.
JEREMIAH 31:3, NASB

Rejoice, the Lord Is King!

Rejoice in glorious hope!

Our Lord the judge shall come,

And take His servants up

To their eternal home:

Lift up your heart, lift up your voice!

Rejoice, again I say, rejoice!

CHARLES WESLEY (1707–1788)

The fascinating thing about God's Word is that we start off learning about Bible characters and end up with a view of *our* character. Moses, Hagar, and Naomi are not distant kin but kissing cousins. I wonder if they're not part of the great cloud of witnesses who are cheering us on, longing for us to learn from their mistakes and triumphs. If we could hear them, what might they say?

Patsy Clairmont, *Under His Wings*

Therefore, since we are surrounded by such a great cloud of witnesses,
let us throw off everything that hinders and the sin that so easily entangles,
and let us run with perseverance the race marked out for us.
Hebrews 12:1, NIV

$\mathcal{A}$ HEALTHY MOTHER-DAUGHTER RELATIONSHIP IS BUILT BY LOVING ONE'S DAUGHTER FOR THE PERSON GOD UNIQUELY CREATED HER TO BE; HONORING HER WITH TIME, ATTENTION, AND AFFECTION; AND GIVING HER TO GOD FOR HIS PURPOSES AND GLORY. Debra Evans, *Kindred Hearts*

For it is God who works in you to will
and to act according to his good purpose.
PHILIPPIANS 2:13, NIV

GOD OF GRACE AND GOD OF GLORY

Set our feet on lofty places,

Gird our lives that they may be

Armored with all Christlike graces

In the fight to set men free.

Grant us wisdom,

Grant us courage,

That we fail not man nor Thee,

That we fail not man nor Thee.

HARRY EMERSON FOSDICK (1878–1969)

Brethren, We Have Met to Worship

Let us love our God supremely,
Let us love each other too;
Let us love and pray for sinners
Till our God makes all things new.
Then He'll call us home to heaven,
At His table we'll sit down;
Christ will gird Himself and serve us
With sweet manna all around.

GEORGE ATKINS (EIGHTEENTH CENTURY)

$\mathcal{G}$OING TO CHURCH TOGETHER AS A FAMILY IS VERY IMPORTANT. IT IS A VITAL WAY FOR US TO ESTABLISH OUR ROOTS, NO MATTER WHERE WE LIVE, FOR IT IS THERE THAT OUR LIFE AS A FAMILY IS ENRICHED. THERE JESUS CHRIST BECOMES THE *CENTER* OF OUR LIVES, NOT JUST A PART.

Susan Miller, *After the Boxes Are Unpacked*

He is before all things, and in Him all things consist.
And He is the head of the body, the church.
COLOSSIANS 1:17-18, NKJV

I Heard the Voice of Jesus Say

I heard the voice of Jesus say,

"Come unto Me and rest;

Lay down, thou weary one, lay down

Thy head upon My breast."

I came to Jesus as I was,

Weary and worn and sad;

I found in Him a resting place,

And He has made me glad.

HORATIUS BONAR (1808–1889)

Saint Augustine said, "Because you have made us for your-self, our hearts are restless until they rest in You." The true rest for our souls, the nourishment we have been seeking from the world, is within reach. We don't have to climb Mount Everest or journey to a rain forest to find this precious commodity. Dr. Deborah Newman, *Then God Created Woman*

Come to me, all you who are weary and burdened,
and I will give you rest.
MATTHEW 11:28, NIV

O PERFECT LOVE

O perfect Love, all human thought transcending,

Lowly we kneel in prayer before Thy throne,

That theirs may be the love which knows no ending,

Whom Thou forevermore dost join in one.

Grant them the joy which brightens earthly sorrow;

Grant them the peace which calms all earthly strife,

And to life's day the glorious unknown morrow

That dawns upon eternal love and life.

DOROTHY FRANCES BLOMFIELD GURNEY (1858–1932)

The marriage relationship is a triangle. The husband serves the wife, and the wife serves the husband. They both serve God equally.

Chuck Snyder, *Men*

Love bears all things, believes all things,
hopes all things, endures all things.
Love never fails.
1 Corinthians 13:4, 7-8, nkjv

EDEEMED

Redeemed and so happy in Jesus,
No language my rapture can tell;
I know that the light of His presence
With me doth continually dwell.

Redeemed, redeemed,
Redeemed by the blood of the Lamb,
Redeemed, redeemed,
His child, and forever, I am.

FANNY JANE CROSBY (1820–1915)

*R*ELATIONSHIP WITH GOD IS ABOUT BEING, NOT DOING. GOD IS MORE CONCERNED THAT WE BE IN RELATIONSHIP WITH HIM THAN THAT WE PERFORM FOR HIM. Dr. Deborah Newman, *Then God Created Woman*

Ye shall seek me, and find me, when ye shall search for me with all your heart.
JEREMIAH 29:13, KJV

COME, LET US RISE
WITH CHRIST

To Him our willing hearts we give
Who gives us power and peace,
And dead to sin, His members live
The life of righteousness;
The hidden life of Christ is ours
With Christ concealed above,
And tasting the celestial powers,
We banquet on His love.

CHARLES WESLEY (1707–1788)

$\mathcal{A}$CCORDING TO THE BIBLE, "LOVE IS THE GREATEST OF THEM ALL," AND IF WE BELIEVE IT, WE WILL MAKE LOVING GOD, OUR FAMILIES, AND ONE ANOTHER THE TOP PRIORITY IN OUR LIVES.

Debra Evans, *Kindred Hearts*

Now abide faith, hope, love, these three;
but the greatest of these is love.
1 CORINTHIANS 13:13, NKJV

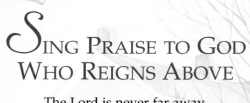

Sing Praise to God Who Reigns Above

The Lord is never far away,

But, through all grief distressing,

An ever-present help and stay,

Our peace and joy and blessing.

As with a mother's tender hand

He leads His own, His chosen band:

To God all praise and glory!

JOHANN JAKOB SCHÜTZ (1640–1690)

TRANSLATED BY FRANCES ELIZABETH COX (1812–1897)

THE WORD *DISCIPLINE* IN THE BIBLE COMES FROM THE SAME ROOT WORD AS *DISCIPLE*. IN OTHER WORDS, WE ARE TO DISCIPLE OUR KIDS IN THE SAME WAY CHRIST DEALT WITH HIS DISCIPLES. THIS MEANS WE'RE TO PARENT WITH PATIENCE, KINDNESS, TENDERNESS, COMPASSION, A LISTENING EAR, A FORGIVING SPIRIT, AND MOST IMPORTANT, *UNCONDITIONAL LOVE*. Chuck Snyder, *Men*

Be ye also patient; stablish your hearts:
for the coming of the Lord draweth nigh.
JAMES 5:8, KJV

ONE OF THE PROBLEMS WITH HAVING A HUMAN REFUGE IS THAT SOMETIMES
THAT PERSON LEAVES. GOD NEVER DOES. Patsy Clairmont, *Under His Wings*

*If you make the Most High your dwelling—
even the Lord, who is my refuge—
then no harm will befall you.*
PSALM 91:9-10, NIV

Take My Life and Let It Be

Take my life and let it be
Consecrated, Lord, to Thee;
Take my moments and my days—
Let them flow in ceaseless praise,
Let them flow in ceaseless praise.

Take my love—my Lord, I pour
At Thy feet its treasure store;
Take myself—and I will be
Ever, only, all for Thee,
Ever, only, all for Thee.

FRANCES RIDLEY HAVERGAL (1836–1879)

My Faith Looks Up to Thee

My faith looks up to Thee,

Thou Lamb of Calvary,

Savior divine!

Now hear me while I pray,

Take all my guilt away,

O let me from this day

Be wholly Thine!

RAY PALMER (1808–1887)

THINK ABOUT WHAT HAPPENS WHEN WE PRAY. FATHER, SON, AND HOLY SPIRIT ARE ALL INVOLVED IN CONVERSATION WITH US! ROMANS 8 SAYS THAT THE HOLY SPIRIT ALSO INTERCEDES ON OUR BEHALF, PUTTING INTO WORDS THE THOUGHTS AND IDEAS THAT ARE TOO DEEP FOR US TO UNDERSTAND OR EXPRESS.

Dr. Deborah Newman, *Then God Created Woman*

Likewise the Spirit also helpeth our infirmities:
for we know not what we should pray for as we ought:
but the Spirit itself maketh intercession for us
with groanings which cannot be uttered.
ROMANS 8:26, KJV

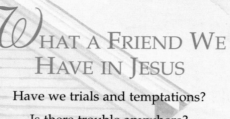

WHAT A FRIEND WE HAVE IN JESUS

Have we trials and temptations?

Is there trouble anywhere?

We should never be discouraged,

Take it to the Lord in prayer.

Can we find a friend so faithful

Who will all our sorrows share?

Jesus knows our every weakness,

Take it to the Lord in prayer.

JOSEPH MEDLICOTT SCRIVEN (1819–1886)

GOD IS BY YOUR SIDE. HE IS THE FRIEND WHO WILL GO WITH YOU. HE WILL EASE YOUR HURT AND BRING YOU CONTENTMENT. HE WILL NEVER LEAVE YOU. HE IS WAITING WITH OPEN ARMS.

Susan Miller, *After the Boxes Are Unpacked*

I will not leave you as orphans; I will come to you.
JOHN 14:18, NASB

HE GIVETH MORE GRACE

He giveth more grace when the burden grows greater;
He sendeth more strength when the labors increase.
To added affliction He addeth His mercy;
To multiplied trials, His multiplied peace.

When we have exhausted our store of endurance,
When our strength has failed ere the day is half done,
When we reach the end of our hoarded resources,
Our Father's full giving is only begun.

ANNIE JOHNSON FLINT (1866–1932)

WE CAN GO THROUGH TRIALS WHEN WE KNOW THAT GOD RULES OVER ALL AND IS IN CONTROL OF EVERY SITUATION. HE USES TRIALS TO MATURE US, TO MAKE US COMPLETE, AND TO MOLD US INTO THE IMAGE OF HIS SON.

Chuck Snyder, *Men*

Let us therefore draw near with confidence to the throne of grace,
that we may receive mercy and may find grace to help in time of need.
HEBREWS 4:16, NASB

DISCOVERING GOD'S LOVE ON EARTH MUST ONLY MAKE MY EXPERIENCE OF MEETING HIM FACE TO FACE MORE MEANINGFUL. GOD DOESN'T JUST WANT ME TO KNOW HOW MUCH HE LOVES ME. HE ALSO YEARNS FOR ME TO LOVE HIM BACK. Dr. Deborah Newman, *Then God Created Woman*

The Father himself loveth you, because ye have loved me,
and have believed that I came out from God.
JOHN 16:27, KJV

GOD IS LOVE; HIS MERCY BRIGHTENS

God is love; His mercy brightens

All the path in which we rove;

Bliss He wakes and woe He lightens:

God is wisdom, God is love.

He with earthly cares entwineth

Hope and comfort from above;

Everywhere His glory shineth:

God is wisdom, God is love.

JOHN BOWRING (1792–1872)

SOLDIERS OF CHRIST, ARISE

Soldiers of Christ, arise,

And put your armor on,

Strong in the strength which God supplies

Through His eternal Son;

Strong in the Lord of hosts,

And in His mighty power,

Who in the strength of Jesus trusts

Is more than conqueror.

CHARLES WESLEY (1707–1788)

$\mathcal{H}$ELP US, LORD! SEND YOUR STRENGTH AND WISDOM. FORGIVE US WHEN WE FALL SHORT, RESTORING US QUICKLY IN YOUR HOLY PRESENCE. GRANT US THE GRACE TO SERVE YOU WITH JOY EACH DAY. MAY WE BE PLEASING TO YOU IN ALL THAT WE DO, THINK, AND SAY. Debra Evans, *Kindred Hearts*

My hope is from Him.
He only is my rock and my salvation, my stronghold;
I shall not be shaken.
PSALM 62:5-6, NASB

I NEED THEE EVERY HOUR

I need Thee ev'ry hour,
Most gracious Lord;
No tender voice like Thine
Can peace afford.

I need Thee, O I need Thee;
Ev'ry hour I need Thee!
O bless me now, my Savior,
I come to Thee.

ANNIE SHERWOOD HAWKS (1835–1918)

ROBERT LOWRY (1826–1899), REFRAIN

I DON'T ALWAYS GET WHAT I WANT FROM THE LORD, BUT HE MEETS ME AT MY NEED. IT MAY BE ONLY ONE WORD, BUT A WORD FROM HIM IS LIFE, AND IT SUSTAINS ME. Patsy Clairmont, *Under His Wings*

The Lord is compassionate and gracious,
slow to anger, abounding in love.
PSALM 103:8, NIV

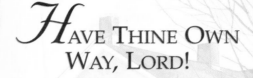

Have Thine Own Way, Lord!

Have Thine own way, Lord! Have Thine own way!
Thou art the potter; I am the clay.
Mold me and make me after Thy will,
While I am waiting, yielded and still.

Have Thine own way, Lord! Have Thine own way!
Hold o'er my being absolute sway!
Fill with Thy Spirit till all shall see
Christ only, always, living in me!

ADELAIDE ADDISON POLLARD (1862–1934)

𝒯HE JOURNEY OF HEALING IS ONE OF ACTION, ACCORDING TO GOD'S PLAN. I
LET GO—GOD MENDS ME. I START OVER—GOD MOLDS ME. I MOVE AHEAD—
GOD MATURES ME. Susan Miller, *After the Boxes Are Unpacked*

Now to Him who is able to do exceeding abundantly
beyond all that we ask or think, according to the power that works within us,
to Him be the glory!
EPHESIANS 3:20-21, NASB

$\mathcal{W}$E ARE LOVED, AND WHEN WE TRULY LOVE, OUR LOVE IS A RESPONSE TO THIS REALITY AND NOT A WAY TO GET LOVE. LOVE THAT IS EARNED IS NOT LOVE AT ALL. WE DON'T EARN GOD'S LOVE. HE GIVES IT TO US.

Dr. Deborah Newman, *Then God Created Woman*

Hereby perceive we the love of God, because he laid down his life for us: and we ought to lay down our lives for the brethren.
1 JOHN 3:16, KJV

ESUS LOVES ME

Jesus loves me! this I know,

For the Bible tells me so;

Little ones to Him belong,

They are weak but He is strong.

Yes, Jesus loves me!

Yes, Jesus loves me!

Yes, Jesus loves me!

The Bible tells me so.

ANNA BARTLETT WARNER (1820–1915)

TRUST AND OBEY

When we walk with the Lord in the light of His Word,

What a glory He sheds on our way!

While we do His good will He abides with us still,

And with all who will trust and obey.

Trust and obey, for there's no other way

To be happy in Jesus, but to trust and obey.

JOHN H. SAMMIS (1846–1919)

WE CAN'T CREATE OUR DAUGHTERS' FAITH FOR THEM—BUT WE *CAN* GIVE OUR DAUGHTERS A REMARKABLE RANGE OF SPIRITUAL STRATEGIES FOR CONFRONTING AND COPING WITH LIFE'S CHALLENGES; WE CAN'T TOTALLY PREDICT THE FINAL OUTCOME OF OUR LONG YEARS OF MOTHERING—BUT WE *CAN* POINT AND GUIDE OUR DAUGHTERS IN THE RIGHT DIRECTION. Debra Evans, *Kindred Hearts*

Teach me to do your will, for you are my God;
may your good Spirit lead me on level ground.
PSALM 143:10, NIV

PRAISE THE SAVIOR, YE WHO KNOW HIM

Praise the Savior, ye who know Him!

Who can tell how much we owe Him?

Gladly let us render to Him

All we are and have.

Jesus is the name that charms us,

He for conflict fits and arms us;

Nothing moves and nothing harms us

While we trust in Him.

THOMAS KELLY (1769–1855)

𝓛EAVE THE RESULTS OF YOUR RELATIONSHIPS TO GOD.

CONTENTMENT DEPENDS ON OUR FOCUS AND HEART ATTITUDE,

NOT ON CIRCUMSTANCES. Chuck Snyder, *Men*

Praise the Lord, O my soul, and forget not all his benefits.
PSALM 103:2, NIV

How Firm a Foundation

How firm a foundation, ye saints of the Lord,

Is laid for your faith in His excellent Word!

What more can He say than to you He hath said,

To you who for refuge to Jesus have fled?

"Fear not, I am with thee; O be not dismayed,

For I am thy God, and will still give thee aid;

I'll strengthen thee, help thee, and cause thee to stand,

Upheld by My righteous, omnipotent hand."

"K" IN RIPPON'S *A SELECTION OF HYMNS*, 1787

$\mathcal{I}$T'S EASY IN THE DAILINESS OF LIFE TO BUY INTO THE MADNESS OF THE WORLD. IT'S IN THE QUIET, AS WE MEET WITH THE GARDENER, THAT HE PULLS THE BRAMBLES OFF OUR BRAINS. THIS ALLOWS SONLIGHT IN AND MOVES US FROM BEING UNINFORMED AND MISINFORMED TO BEING TRANSFORMED AND CONFORMED—TRANSFORMED IN OUR THINKING AND CONFORMED TO THE IMAGE OF CHRIST. Patsy Clairmont, *Under His Wings*

Be still, and know that I am God;
I will be exalted among the nations,
I will be exalted in the earth!
PSALM 46:10, NKJV

As Christ's lordship enlarges to cover every area of your life, you will find the peace, joy, and freedom He promises to His followers. It's guaranteed. Debra Evans, *Kindred Hearts*

You have made known to me the ways of life;
You will make me full of joy in Your presence.
Acts 2:28, NKJV

$\mathcal{M}$Y JESUS, I LOVE THEE

My Jesus, I love Thee, I know Thou art mine—
For Thee all the follies of sin I resign;
My gracious Redeemer, my Savior art Thou:
If ever I loved Thee, my Jesus, 'tis now.

In mansions of glory and endless delight,
I'll ever adore Thee in heaven so bright;
I'll sing with the glittering crown on my brow,
"If ever I loved Thee, my Jesus, 'tis now."

WILLIAM RALPH FEATHERSTON (1846–1873)

DAY BY DAY AND WITH EACH PASSING MOMENT

Help me then in ev'ry tribulation
So to trust Thy promises, O Lord,
That I lose not faith's sweet consolation
Offered me within Thy holy Word.
Help me, Lord, when toil and trouble meeting,
E'er to take, as from a father's hand,
One by one, the days, the moments fleeting,
Till I reach the promised land.

CAROLINA SANDELL BERG (1832–1903)

TRANSLATED BY ANDREW L. SKOOG (1856–1934)

WOMEN WHO ARE OVERCOMERS HOLD THESE THINGS IN COMMON: THEIR UNWAVERING FAITH IN JESUS CHRIST. THEIR INNER STRENGTH COMES FROM HIM. THEIR ENDURING PERSEVERANCE IS A RESULT OF KNOWING JESUS AS THEIR LORD. Susan Miller, *After the Boxes Are Unpacked*

I can do all things through Christ who strengthens me.
PHILIPPIANS 4:13, NKJV

BREATHE ON ME, BREATH OF GOD

Breathe on me, Breath of God,

Fill me with life anew,

That I may love what Thou dost love,

And do what Thou wouldst do.

Breathe on me, Breath of God,

Till I am wholly Thine,

Till all this earthly part of me

Glows with Thy fire divine.

EDWIN HATCH (1835–1889)

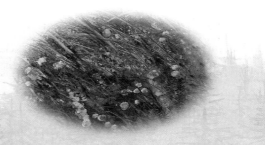

"THE LOVE OF GOD IS NOT MERE SENTIMENTALITY; IT IS THE MOST PRACTICAL THING FOR THE SAINTS TO LOVE AS GOD LOVES. THE SPRINGS OF LOVE ARE IN GOD, NOT IN US," OBSERVED SCOTTISH EVANGELIST OSWALD CHAMBERS. BY VIEWING OUR DAUGHTERS FROM THE CREATOR'S PERSPECTIVE—AND RELYING UPON HIS GRACE TO RENEW OUR VISION DAY BY DAY—WE CAN MIRROR THEIR SPECIAL QUALITIES BACK TO THEM. Debra Evans, *Kindred Hearts*

We all, with unveiled face, beholding as in a mirror the glory of the Lord, are being transformed into the same image from glory to glory, just as by the Spirit of the Lord.
2 CORINTHIANS 3:18, NKJV

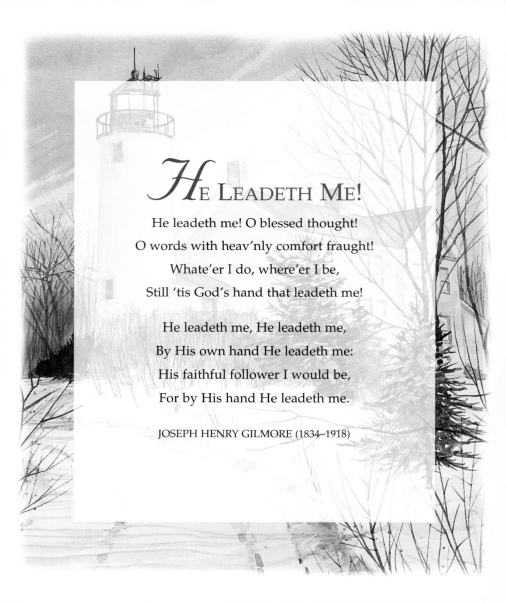

HE LEADETH ME!

He leadeth me! O blessed thought!
O words with heav'nly comfort fraught!
Whate'er I do, where'er I be,
Still 'tis God's hand that leadeth me!

He leadeth me, He leadeth me,
By His own hand He leadeth me:
His faithful follower I would be,
For by His hand He leadeth me.

JOSEPH HENRY GILMORE (1834–1918)

ONE OF A MAN'S GREATEST GIFTS TO HIS WIFE IS LISTENING—BECAUSE THAT MEANS HE VALUES THE RELATIONSHIP ENOUGH TO SHARE HIS WORLD WITH HER!

Chuck Snyder, *Men*

He who listens to me shall live securely,
and shall be at ease from the dread of evil.
PROVERBS 1:33, NASB

THERE'S NOTHING THAT PLEASES GOD MORE THAN WHEN I ADMIT I'VE BLOWN IT. HE DOESN'T WANT ME TO TRY TO BE THE BEST PERSON IN THE WORLD IN MY OWN STRENGTH. HE LONGS FOR ME TO REALIZE MY LIMITATIONS AND COME TO HIM JUST AS I AM. WHEN I ADMIT MY WEAKNESS AND BROKENNESS, ONLY THEN AM I TRULY STRONG, JUST AS PAUL SAID (2 COR. 12:10).

Dr. Deborah Newman, *Then God Created Woman*

*Follow after righteousness, godliness, faith, love, patience, meekness.
Fight the good fight of faith, lay hold on eternal life
whereunto thou art also called, and hast professed a good profession
before many witnesses.*
1 TIMOTHY 6:11-12, KJV

ℱIGHT THE GOOD FIGHT

Fight the good fight with all thy might!

Christ is thy strength, and Christ thy right.

Lay hold on life, and it shall be

Thy joy and crown eternally.

Run the straight race through God's good grace;

Lift up thine eyes, and seek His face.

Life with its way before us lies;

Christ is the path, and Christ the prize.

JOHN SAMUEL BEWLEY MONSELL (1811–1875)

OPEN MY EYES, THAT I MAY SEE

Open my eyes, that I may see

Glimpses of truth Thou hast for me;

Place in my hands the wonderful key,

That shall unclasp and set me free.

Silently now I wait for Thee,

Ready, my God, Thy will to see;

Open my eyes, illumine me,

Spirit divine!

CLARA H. SCOTT (1841–1897)

$\mathcal{G}$OD CALLS US TO COME UP HIGHER SO WE, TOO, CAN GAIN A HOLIER PERSPECTIVE AND CATCH A GLIMPSE OF THE PROMISED LAND.

Patsy Clairmont, *Under His Wings*

Do good to your servant, and I will live; I will obey your word.
Open my eyes that I may see wonderful things in your law.
I am a stranger on earth; do not hide your commands from me.
My soul is consumed with longing for your laws at all times.
PSALM 119:17-20, NIV

O Master, Let Me Walk with Thee

O Master, let me walk with Thee

In lowly paths of service free;

Tell me Thy secret; help me bear

The strain of toil, the fret of care.

Teach me Thy patience; still with Thee

In closer, dearer company,

In work that keeps faith sweet

and strong,

In trust that triumphs over wrong.

WASHINGTON GLADDEN (1836–1918)

I BELIEVE GOD CALLS US TO PURSUE EXCELLENCE FOR HIS GLORY IN

EVERY AREA OF OUR LIVES—TO AIM TO DO OUR BEST WITH THE

TALENTS, RESOURCES, TIME, SKILLS, AND TOOLS HE GIVES US.

Debra Evans, *Kindred Hearts*

Whatever is true, whatever is noble, whatever is right,
whatever is pure, whatever is lovely, whatever is admirable—
if anything is excellent or praiseworthy—think about such things.
PHILIPPIANS 4:8, NIV

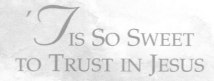

'Tis So Sweet to Trust in Jesus

'Tis so sweet to trust in Jesus,

Just to take Him at His Word,

Just to rest upon His promise,

Just to know "Thus saith the Lord."

Jesus, Jesus, how I trust Him!

How I've proved Him o'er and o'er!

Jesus, Jesus, precious Jesus!

O for grace to trust Him more!

LOUISA M. R. STEAD (1850–1917)

$\mathcal{G}$OD HAS TAUGHT ME SOMETHING IMPORTANT THROUGH EVERY MOVE, EVERY HOUSE, AND EVERY PLACE WE'VE LIVED: MY SECURITY DOES NOT COME FROM A HOUSE (OR ANY OTHER THING, FOR THAT MATTER). REAL SECURITY COMES ONLY FROM TRUSTING IN GOD. Susan Miller, *After the Boxes Are Unpacked*

I will say to the Lord, "My refuge and my fortress,
my God, in whom I trust!"
PSALM 91:2, NASB

BEGIN, MY TONGUE, SOME HEAVENLY THEME

Begin, my tongue, some heav'nly theme

And speak some boundless thing:

The mighty works or mightier name

Of our eternal King.

Tell of His wondrous faithfulness

And sound His pow'r abroad;

Sing the sweet promise of His grace,

The love and truth of God.

ISAAC WATTS (1674–1748)

Coming together in marriage is like two streams flowing side by side and then blending. When the streams come together, there is a great deal of foam and splashing. However, as they become one, they are stronger and deeper than either one of them was individually.

Chuck Snyder, *Men*

*For this reason a man will leave his father and mother
and be united to his wife, and they will become one flesh.*
Genesis 2:24, NIV

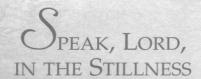

SPEAK, LORD,
IN THE STILLNESS

Speak, Lord, in the stillness,

While I wait on Thee;

Hush my heart to listen

In expectancy.

All to Thee is yielded,

I am not my own;

Blissful, glad surrender,

I am Thine alone.

EMILY MAY GRIMES (1868–1927)

*P*ATIENCE MEANS "BE QUIET AND WAIT." THESE ARE RADICAL, LIFE-CHANGING WORDS—A PROMISE FOR HELP AND HOLY INTERVENTION IN THE MIDST OF OUR HECTIC, HIGH-STRESS LIVES. WHERE WE ARE LACKING, GOD GIVES US HIS PLEDGE THAT HE WILL UNFAILINGLY SUPPLY OUR NEEDS. Debra Evans, *Kindred Hearts*

In quietness and confidence shall be your strength.
ISAIAH 30:15, NKJV

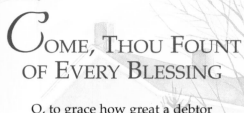

COME, THOU FOUNT OF EVERY BLESSING

O, to grace how great a debtor

Daily I'm constrained to be!

Let that grace, Lord, like a fetter,

Bind my wand'ring heart to Thee.

Prone to wander, Lord, I feel it;

Prone to leave the God I love;

Here's my heart; Lord, take and seal it;

Seal it for Thy courts above.

ROBERT ROBINSON (1735–1790)

$\mathscr{A}$s we spend time with the Lord to get our thoughts straight, to allow Him to touch the painful issues of our hearts, and to accept the truth that much of life is outside our control—but not His—we will begin to see measurable progress in our personal journey.

Patsy Clairmont, *Under His Wings*

Call to Me, and I will answer you,
and I will tell you great and mighty things, which you do not know.
JEREMIAH 33:3, NASB

$\mathcal{I}$T TAKES A LOT OF FAITH TO FACE THE UNKNOWN. BUT WHAT A COMFORT IT IS TO KNOW THAT GOD PROMISES NOT TO LEAVE US OR FORSAKE US (DEUT. 31:8). MY FAITH IS WRAPPED AROUND GOD'S PROMISES IN SCRIPTURE.

Susan Miller, *After the Boxes Are Unpacked*

> *I will never leave thee, nor forsake thee.*
> HEBREWS 13:5, KJV

I Am Not Skilled to Understand

I am not skilled to understand
What God hath willed, what God hath planned;
I only know at His right hand
Stands One who is my Savior.

And O that He fulfilled may see
The travail of His soul in me,
And with His work contented be,
As I with my dear Savior!

DORA GREENWELL (1821–1882)

CLOSE TO THEE

Not for ease or worldly pleasure,

Nor for fame my prayer shall be;

Gladly will I toil and suffer,

Only let me walk with Thee.

Close to Thee, close to Thee,

Close to Thee, close to Thee;

Gladly will I toil and suffer,

Only let me walk with Thee.

FANNY JANE CROSBY (1820–1915)

A CONTENTED WOMAN HAS A HEALTHY, BALANCED VIEW OF GOD THAT ENHANCES HER VALUE IN THE CHURCH AND IN SOCIETY. SHE ISN'T PERFECT, BUT HER DEEP RELATIONSHIP WITH GOD HAS TRANSFORMED HER PAIN AND PERSONALITY. IN THE FREEDOM OF HIS LOVE, SHE HAS DISCOVERED HER UNIQUENESS AND IS EAGER TO FOLLOW HIS DIRECTION FOR LIVING IN THIS WORLD.

Dr. Deborah Newman, *Then God Created Woman*

As ye have therefore received Christ Jesus the Lord,
so walk ye in him: rooted and built up in him, and stablished in the faith,
as ye have been taught, abounding therein with thanksgiving.
COLOSSIANS 2:6-7, KJV

Jesus, Priceless Treasure

Jesus, priceless treasure,

Source of purest pleasure,

Truest friend to me,

Long my heart hath panted,

Till it well-nigh fainted,

Thirsting after Thee.

Thine I am, O spotless Lamb.

I will suffer naught to hide Thee,

Ask for naught beside Thee.

JOHANN FRANCK (1618–1677)

TRANSLATED BY

CATHERINE WINKWORTH (1827–1878)

WE ARE NOT DESIGNED TO DEPEND ON HUMAN FANTASIES AND IDEALS, BUT ON
GOD ALONE, AS OUR SOLE SOURCE OF LIFE, HOPE, STRENGTH, AND VISION.
SUBSTITUTES, NO MATTER WHO OR WHAT THEY ARE, WILL NEVER SATISFY US.
WE ARE DESIGNED TO HUNGER AFTER THE FRUITS OF THE HOLY SPIRIT INSTEAD.

Debra Evans, *Kindred Hearts*

*The fruit of the Spirit is love, joy, peace, patience, kindness,
goodness, faithfulness, gentleness and self-control.*
GALATIANS 5:22-23, NIV

$\mathscr{B}$LEST BE THE DEAR UNITING LOVE

Blest be the dear uniting love

That will not let us part;

Our bodies may far off remove,

We still are one in heart.

Partakers of the Savior's grace,

The same in mind and heart,

Nor joy, nor grief, nor time, nor place,

Nor life, nor death can part.

CHARLES WESLEY (1707–1788)

The helpmeet (completion) idea in Genesis 2:18 speaks to me of equality. My wife completes me and brings gifts and character strengths to our relationship that I don't have. I complete her and bring gifts and character strengths to our relationship that she doesn't have. We both submit ourselves to God and become *one* flesh; inseparable, indivisible; a single entity. Chuck Snyder, *Men*

May the God who gives endurance and encouragement give you
a spirit of unity among yourselves as you follow Christ Jesus.
Romans 15:5, NIV

When we have done all we humanly know to do, we have no choice but to wait on God. The rock-hard place of believing without seeing holds the potential for great growth in our lives.

Patsy Clairmont, *Under His Wings*

It is good that one should hope and wait quietly for the salvation of the Lord.
LAMENTATIONS 3:26, NKJV

A WONDERFUL SAVIOR IS JESUS MY LORD

A wonderful Savior is Jesus my Lord,
He taketh my burden away;
He holdeth me up, and I shall not be moved,
He giveth me strength as my day.

He hideth my soul in the cleft of the rock
That shadows a dry, thirsty land;
He hideth my life in the depths of His love,
And covers me there with His hand.
And covers me there with His hand.

FANNY JANE CROSBY (1820–1915)

Savior, Like a Shepherd Lead Us

Savior, like a shepherd lead us,
Much we need Thy tender care;
In Thy pleasant pastures feed us,
For our use Thy folds prepare:
Blessed Jesus, blessed Jesus!
Thou has bought us, Thine we are.

HYMNS FOR THE YOUNG, 1836

ATTRIBUTED TO DOROTHY A. THRUPP (1779–1847)

GOD IS THE ONE WHO CLASPS YOUR HAND AS YOU MOVE FROM ONE PLACE TO ANOTHER. HE IS THE ONE WHO HAS GONE AHEAD OF YOU, PREPARED A PLACE FOR YOU, AND WILL HOLD OUT HIS HAND FOR YOU TO CLING TO.

Susan Miller, *After the Boxes Are Unpacked*

For I am the Lord, your God,
who takes hold of your right hand and says to you,
Do not fear; I will help you.
ISAIAH 41:13, NIV

Guide Me, O Thou Great Jehovah

Guide me, O Thou great Jehovah,

Pilgrim through this barren land;

I am weak, but Thou art mighty;

Hold me with Thy powerful hand;

Bread of heaven, Bread of heaven,

Feed me till I want no more.

Feed me till I want no more.

WILLIAM WILLIAMS (1717–1791)

STANZA TRANSLATED FROM THE WELSH

BY PETER WILLIAMS (1722–1796)

GOD IS A JUST, LOVING, ALL-POWERFUL, ALL-KNOWING HEALER, RULER, FRIEND, AND GUIDE. HE USES NUMEROUS CHARACTERISTICS TO DESCRIBE HIMSELF IN SCRIPTURE.

Dr. Deborah Newman, *Then God Created Woman*

For this is God, our God forever and ever;
He will be our guide even to death.
PSALM 48:14, NKJV

WONDERFUL GRACE OF JESUS

Wonderful grace of Jesus,
Reaching the most defiled,
By its transforming power
Making me God's dear child,
Purchasing peace and heaven
For all eternity—
And the wonderful grace of Jesus reaches me.

HALDOR LILLENAS (1885–1959)

$\mathcal{Y}$OU CAN TRANSFORM YOUR MARRIAGE ALL BY YOURSELF JUST BY BEING THE

MATE GOD WANTS YOU TO BE. Chuck Snyder, *Men*

*Do not be conformed to this world, but be transformed
by the renewing of your mind, that you may prove what
is that good and acceptable and perfect will of God.*
ROMANS 12:2, NKJV

𝑀OSES WASN'T AN OVERNIGHT WONDER. HE STUMBLED AND GRUMBLED JUST AS I DID—AND STILL DO AT TIMES. YET EVENTUALLY HE FOUND HIS WAY TO THE MOUNTAINTOP AND, MORE IMPORTANTLY, INTO THE SHELTERING PRESENCE OF THE LORD. AND WE CAN DO THE SAME. Patsy Clairmont, *Under His Wings*

Thou art my hiding place and my shield; I wait for Thy word.
PSALM 119:113-114, NASB

O GOD, OUR HELP IN AGES PAST

O God, our help in ages past,
Our hope for years to come,
Our shelter from the stormy blast,
And our eternal home!

Under the shadow of Thy throne
Still may we dwell secure;
Sufficient is Thine arm alone,
And our defense is sure.

ISAAC WATTS (1674–1748)

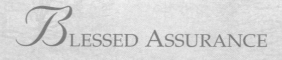 Blessed Assurance

Blessed assurance, Jesus is mine!
O what a foretaste of glory divine!
Heir of salvation, purchase of God,
Born of His Spirit, washed in His blood.

This is my story, this is my song,
Praising my Savior all the day long;
This is my story, this is my song,
Praising my Savior all the day long.

FANNY JANE CROSBY (1820–1915)

GOD WAS WITH YOU WHEN YOU STARTED, AND WILL BE WITH YOU WHEN YOU FINISH. IF YOU SHOULD FALL ALONG THE WAY, HE WILL BE THERE TO PROTECT AND GUIDE YOU, AND MAKE SURE YOU KEEP GOING! THANK YOU, GOD, FOR THIS BLESSED ASSURANCE! Susan Miller, *After the Boxes Are Unpacked*

The Lord is your keeper. . . . He will keep your soul.
The Lord will guard your going out and
your coming in from this time forth and forever.
PSALM 121:5-8, NASB

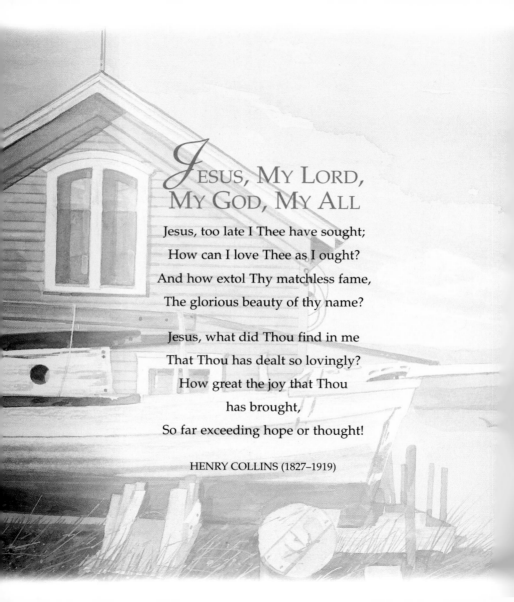

JESUS, MY LORD, MY GOD, MY ALL

Jesus, too late I Thee have sought;

How can I love Thee as I ought?

And how extol Thy matchless fame,

The glorious beauty of thy name?

Jesus, what did Thou find in me

That Thou has dealt so lovingly?

How great the joy that Thou

has brought,

So far exceeding hope or thought!

HENRY COLLINS (1827–1919)

$\mathcal{G}$OD PROMISES THAT HE WILL BE FOUND. JEREMIAH 29:11-14 AND 2 CHRONICLES 7:14 ARE PROMISES THAT IF WE SEEK HIM, HE WILL REVEAL HIMSELF TO US. THIS DOES NOT MEAN THAT WE WILL GET INSTANT ANSWERS OR INSTANT RELIEF. IT IS OUR CONSISTENT DESIRE TO SEE HIM FOR WHO HE IS THAT CLARIFIES OUR VISION OF HIM.

Dr. Deborah Newman, *Then God Created Woman*

If my people, who are called by my name,
will humble themselves and pray and seek my face
and turn from their wicked ways,
then will I hear from heaven and will forgive
their sin and will heal their land.
2 CHRONICLES 7:14, NIV

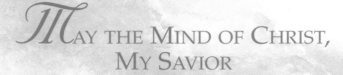

MAY THE MIND OF CHRIST, MY SAVIOR

May the mind of Christ, my Savior,

Live in me from day to day,

By His love and pow'r controlling

All I do and say.

May the word of God dwell richly

In my heart from hour to hour,

So that all may see I triumph

Only through His pow'r.

KATE B. WILKINSON (1859–1928)

$\mathcal{W}$HEN HARD THINGS HAPPEN, TRY THE FOLLOWING STEPS:

CALL UPON THE LORD. (REMEMBER WHO'S IN CONTROL.)

CALM YOUR BODY. (RELAX.)

COLLECT YOUR THOUGHTS. (RENEW YOUR MIND.)

CARRY ON QUIETLY. (RESTORE YOUR SCHEDULE.)

Patsy Clairmont, *Under His Wings*

Be renewed in the spirit of your mind.
EPHESIANS 4:23, NKJV

$\mathcal{G}$OD "WEAVES IN" HIS PROMISES, HIS HOPE, HIS EVERLASTING LOVE, AND HIS MERCY TO STRENGTHEN THE ROPE OF HIS FAITHFULNESS, HIS WORD, AND MOST OF ALL, CONSTANT PRAYER. IT CANNOT BE PULLED APART. THE THREADS OF YOUR LIFE HAVE BEEN WOVEN TOGETHER INTO A ROPE STRONG ENOUGH TO CARRY YOU. JUST REMEMBER THAT WHEN YOU NEED IT, THE ROPE WILL HOLD.

Susan Miller, *After the Boxes Are Unpacked*

Strengthen me according to Thy word.
PSALM 119:28, NASB

ℙRAISE HIM! PRAISE HIM!

Praise Him! praise Him! Jesus, our blessed Redeeemer!

Sing, O Earth, His wonderful love proclaim!

Hail Him! hail Him! highest archangels in glory;

Strength and honor give to His holy name!

Like a shepherd Jesus will guard His children,

In His arms He carries them all day long:

Praise Him! praise Him! tell of His excellent greatness;

Praise Him! praise Him! ever in joyful song!

FANNY JANE CROSBY (1820–1915)

Come, We That Love the Lord

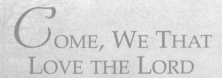

Come, we that love the Lord,
And let our joys be known;
Join in a song with sweet accord,
And thus surround the throne.

Let those refuse to sing
Who never knew our God;
But children of the heav'nly King
May speak their joys abroad.

ISAAC WATTS (1674–1748)

SOMETHING LIBERATING AND HEALING HAPPENS INSIDE US WHEN WE RELINQUISH OUR RIGHT TO UNDERSTAND AND OBEY GOD'S SEEMINGLY OUTRAGEOUS REQUESTS. SUCH JOY CAN COME OVER US THAT IT'S ALL WE CAN DO NOT TO SHOUT. Patsy Clairmont, *Under His Wings*

*Give thanks to the Lord for his unfailing love
and his wonderful deeds for men, for he satisfies the thirsty
and fills the hungry with good things.*
PSALM 107:8-9, NIV

OUT OF THE DEPTHS I CRY TO THEE

Thou canst be merciful while just,

This is my hope's foundation;

In Thy redeeming grace I trust,

O grant me Thy salvation.

Upheld by Thee I stand secure:

Thy word is firm, Thy promise sure,

And I rely upon Thee.

MARTIN LUTHER (1483–1546)

TRANSLATED BY BENJAMIN LATROBE (1725–1786)

$\mathcal{N}$O MATTER WHERE YOU'VE BEEN, WHERE YOU ARE, OR WHERE YOU ARE GOING, KNOWING JESUS CHRIST CAN CHANGE THE COURSE OF YOUR LIFE.

Susan Miller, *After the Boxes Are Unpacked*

He who believes in the Son has everlasting life.
JOHN 3:36, NKJV

$\mathcal{I}$T IS ONLY IN BELIEVING THAT WE ARE LOVED WITH AN EVERLASTING LOVE
THAT WE BEGIN TO LEAVE OUR FEARS BEHIND AND EXPERIENCE GREAT JOY AT
THE THOUGHT OF GETTING TO KNOW OUR CREATOR BETTER.

Dr. Deborah Newman, *Then God Created Woman*

There is no fear in love; but perfect love casteth out fear.
1 JOHN 4:18, KJV

FOR THE BEAUTY OF THE EARTH

For the beauty of the earth,

For the glory of the skies,

For the love which from our birth

Over and around us lies:

Lord of all, to Thee we raise

This our hymn of grateful praise.

FOLLIOT SANFORD PIERPOINT (1835–1917)

HAPPY THE HOME WHEN GOD IS THERE

Happy the home when God is there,

And love fills every breast;

When one their wish, and one their prayer,

And one their heavenly rest.

Happy the home where Jesus' name

Is sweet to every ear;

Where children early lisp His fame,

And parents hold Him dear.

HENRY WARE JR. (1794–1843)

$\mathcal{P}$ARENTS ARE BLESSED TO BE CHOSEN BY $\mathcal{G}$OD TO SPEND 24 HOURS A DAY, SEVEN DAYS A WEEK, 365 DAYS A YEAR WITH THEIR KIDS. WHAT A PRICELESS PRIVILEGE TO BE CALLED *PARENTS!* Chuck Snyder, *Men*

She looketh well to the ways of her household, and eateth not the bread of idleness.
Her children arise up, and call her blessed; her husband also, and he praiseth her.
PROVERBS 31:27-28, KJV

I Sing the Mighty Power of God

There's not a plant or flow'r below,

But makes Thy glories known:

And clouds arise, and tempests blow,

By order from Thy throne;

While all that borrows life from Thee

Is ever in Thy care.

And ev'rywhere that man can be,

Thou, God, art present there.

ISAAC WATTS (1674–1748)

$\mathcal{N}$EVER FORGET, THE ROAD HAS BEEN TRAVELED BEFORE YOU. THE CHOICE TO CHERISH THE PAST AND CLING TO GOD FOR THE FUTURE IS NOT ALWAYS EASY, BUT FAITH, HOPE, PERSEVERANCE, PRAYER, AND OBEDIENCE ARE THE KEYS. Susan Miller, *After the Boxes Are Unpacked*

Be strong in the Lord and in the power of His might.
Stand therefore, having girded your waist with truth,
having put on the breastplate of righteousness.
EPHESIANS 6:10, 14, NKJV

Jesus, I Am Resting, Resting

Jesus, I am resting, resting
In the joy of what Thou art;
I am finding out the greatness
Of Thy loving heart.
Thou hast bid me gaze upon Thee,
And Thy beauty fills my soul,
For by Thy transforming power,
Thou hast made me whole.

JEAN SOPHIA PIGOTT (1845–1882)

$\mathcal{A}$ LIFE OF LOVE IS ONLY POSSIBLE BY GETTING IN TOUCH WITH THE ONE WHO TRULY LOVES US. THE CLOSER I GET TO GOD'S HEART, THE MORE I WANT TO LOVE OTHERS. I LONG TO LOVE BECAUSE I HAVE BEEN SO DEEPLY LOVED.

Dr. Deborah Newman, *Then God Created Woman*

Let love and faithfulness never leave you;
bind them around your neck, write them on the tablet of your heart.
Then you will win favor and a good name in the sight of God and man.
PROVERBS 3:3-4, NIV

When we feel discouraged, we can choose to turn to God for strength and peace. When we are in turmoil, we can ask Him to comfort us and remind us of His grace. We can accept the freedom Christ offers us day by day through His cleansing forgiveness and unconditional love. Debra Evans, *Kindred Hearts*

May the God of all grace, who called us to His eternal glory by Christ Jesus, after you have suffered a while, perfect, establish, strengthen, and settle you. To Him be the glory and the dominion forever and ever. Amen.
1 Peter 5:10-11, NKJV

DEPTH OF MERCY!

Depth of mercy! can there be
Mercy still reserved for me?
Can my God His wrath forbear,
Me, the chief of sinners, spare?

There for me the Savior stands,
Holding forth His wounded hands;
God is love! I know, I feel,
Jesus weeps and loves me still.

CHARLES WESLEY (1707–1788)

LIKE A RIVER GLORIOUS

Like a river glorious
Is God's perfect peace,
Over all victorious
In its bright increase;
Perfect, yet it floweth
Fuller ev'ry day,
Perfect, yet it groweth
Deeper all the way.

FRANCES RIDLEY HAVERGAL (1836–1879)

PRAYER IS THE STARTING POINT THAT OPENS THE DOOR TO GOD AND LETTING HIM WORK IN HIS TIME. AS WE LOOK TO HIM AND HONESTLY ADMIT, "I CAN'T DO THIS, LORD!" HE STRETCHES OUT HIS HANDS AND PROVIDES THE PROMISE OF PEACE. HE IS THE ONLY EVERLASTING SOURCE OF QUIETNESS AND PATIENCE.

Debra Evans, *Kindred Hearts*

To the Lord I cry aloud, and he answers me from his holy hill.
PSALM 3:4, NIV

HOLY BIBLE, BOOK DIVINE

Holy Bible, book divine,

Precious treasure, thou art mine;

Mine to tell me whence I came;

Mine to teach me what I am.

Mine to comfort in distress,

Suff'ring in this wilderness;

Mine to show, by living faith,

Man can triumph over death.

JOHN BURTON (1773–1822)

The more you know and study God's Word, the firmer the ground upon which you stand will be. God's Word will keep you on track with His truth and His promises. Susan Miller, *After the Boxes Are Unpacked*

Your word is a lamp to my feet
and a light for my path.
PSALM 119:105, NIV

All Praise to Thee, My God, This Night

All praise to Thee, my God, this night,
For all the blessings of the light!
Keep me, O keep me, King of kings,
Beneath Thine own almighty wings.

Praise God, from whom all blessings flow;
Praise Him, all creatures here below;
Praise Him above, ye heavenly host;
Praise Father, Son, and Holy Ghost.

THOMAS KEN (1637–1711)

$\mathcal{I}$ LIKE THE ANSWER GOD GAVE THE AUTHOR OF THE FAMOUS "FOOTPRINTS" POEM WHEN SHE ASKED HIM WHY SHE SAW HIS FOOTPRINTS BESIDE HER DURING THE EASY TIMES OF LIFE BUT NOT WHEN TIMES WERE ROUGH. HE TOLD HER, "THAT WAS WHEN I CARRIED YOU." HE GIVES THE SAME ANSWER TO US. WE MUST REMEMBER THAT HE IS ALWAYS WITH US.

Dr. Deborah Newman, *Then God Created Woman*

*For the Lord will be your confidence,
and will keep your foot from being caught.*
PROVERBS 3:26, NASB

THERE ARE SOME THINGS WE CAN'T DO, CHANGE, OR UNDERSTAND, AND

THOSE ARE GOD'S PARTS TO TAKE CARE OF. Patsy Clairmont, *Under His Wings*

He who searches our hearts knows the mind of the Spirit,
because the Spirit intercedes for the saints in accordance with God's will.
ROMANS 8:27, NIV

Blessed Jesus, at Thy Word

Glorious Lord, Thyself impart,
Light of Light, from God proceeding;
Open Thou our ears and heart,
Help us by Thy Spirit's pleading;
Hear the cry Thy people raises,
Hear and bless our prayers and praises.

TOBIAS CLAUSNITZER (1619–1684)

TRANSLATED BY CATHERINE WINKWORTH (1827–1878)

SPIRIT OF GOD,
DESCEND UPON MY HEART

Spirit of God, descend upon my heart;

Wean it from earth; through all its pulses move;

Stoop to my weakness, mighty as Thou art,

And make me love Thee as I ought to love.

Teach me to feel that Thou art always nigh;

Teach me the struggles of the soul to bear,

To check the rising doubt, the rebel sigh;

Teach me the patience of unanswered prayer.

GEORGE CROLY (1780–1860)

*P*RAYER IS THE VEHICLE WE USE TO TRANSPORT THE LOADS THAT WEIGH HEAVILY ON OUR HEARTS, LEAVING THEM AT THE FOOT OF THE CROSS. IN PRAYER, WE TURN TO FACE GOD AS WE ARE, WITH LONGING, HUNGER, AND THIRST, ASKING TO BE FILLED AGAIN. Debra Evans, *Kindred Hearts*

Blessed are they which do hunger and thirst after righteousness:
for they shall be filled.
MATTHEW 5:6, KJV

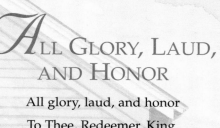

ALL GLORY, LAUD, AND HONOR

All glory, laud, and honor

To Thee, Redeemer, King,

To whom the lips of children

Made sweet hosannas ring:

Thou art the King of Israel,

Thou David's royal Son,

Who in the Lord's name comest,

The King and blessed One!

THEODULF OF ORLÉANS (C. 750–821)

TRANSLATED BY

JOHN MASON NEALE (1818–1866)

CHILDREN ARE A GIFT FROM GOD AND NEED LOTS OF TENDER,

LOVING CARE. Chuck Snyder, *Men*

From everlasting to everlasting the Lord's love is with those who fear him,
and his righteousness with their children's children—
with those who keep his covenant and remember to obey his precepts.
PSALM 103:17-18, NIV

TEACH ME, O LORD, THY HOLY WAY

Teach me, O Lord, Thy holy way,

And give me an obedient mind;

That in Thy service I may find

My soul's delight from day to day.

Guide me, O Savior, with Thy hand,

And so control my thoughts and deeds,

That I may tread the path which leads

Right onward to the blessed land.

WILLIAM T. MATSON (1833–1899)

$\mathcal{W}$HEN WE DECIDE TO BE HIS, WE BECOME LESS RESISTANT TO THE WEEDING AND PRUNING AND MORE SINGLE-MINDED IN OUR FOCUS ON THE PATH AHEAD. GROWTH COMES DOWN TO THIS QUESTION: ARE WE WILLING TO HEAR, LEARN, AND CHANGE? Patsy Clairmont, *Under His Wings*

I, the Lord, search the heart, I test the mind,
even to give to each man according to his ways,
according to the results of his deeds.
JEREMIAH 17:10, NASB

$\mathcal{W}$ELCOME TO THE FAMILY!

Whether you received this book as a gift, borrowed it from a friend, or purchased it yourself, we're glad you read it! It's just one of the many helpful, insightful, and encouraging resources produced by Focus on the Family.

In fact, that's what Focus on the Family is all about—providing inspiration, information, and biblically based advice to people in all stages of life.

It began in 1977 with the vision of one man, Dr. James Dobson, a licensed psychologist and best-selling author. Now an international organization, Focus on the Family is dedicated to preserving Judeo-Christian values and strengthening the family through more than seventy different ministries, including eight separate radio broadcasts; television public-service announcements; eleven publications; and a steady series of books and award-winning films and videos for people of all ages and interests. And it's all done for one purpose: to encourage and strengthen individuals and families through the life-changing message of Jesus Christ.

For more information about the ministry, or if we can be of help to your family, simply write to Focus on the Family, Colorado Springs, CO 80995 or call 1-800-A-FAMILY (1-800-232-6459). Friends in Canada may write to Focus on the Family, P.O. Box 9800, Stn. Terminal, Vancouver, B.C. V6B 4G3 or call 1-800-661-9800. You may also visit our Web site—www.family.org—to learn more about the ministry or to find out if there is a Focus on the Family office in your country.